94

THINGS TO DO
AT HOME DURING
THE CORONAVIRUS

DAVID LARIVIERE

BALBOA.PRESS

A DIVISION OF HAY HOUSE

Balboa Press books may be ordered through booksellers or by contacting:

Balboa Press
A Division of Hay House
1663 Liberty Drive
Bloomington, IN 47403
www.balboapress.com
1 (877) 407-4847

Because of the dynamic nature of the Internet, any web addresses or links contained in this book may have changed since publication and may no longer be valid. The views expressed in this work are solely those of the author and do not necessarily reflect the views of the publisher, and the publisher hereby disclaims any responsibility for them.

The author of this book does not dispense medical advice or prescribe the use of any technique as a form of treatment for physical, emotional, or medical problems without the advice of a physician, either directly or indirectly. The intent of the author is only to offer information of a general nature to help you in your quest for emotional and spiritual well-being. In the event you use any of the information in this book for yourself, which is your constitutional right, the author and the publisher assume no responsibility for your actions.

Any people depicted in stock imagery provided by Getty Images are models, and such images are being used for illustrative purposes only. Certain stock imagery © Getty Images.

Print information available on the last page.

ISBN: 978-1-9822-4820-8 (sc)
ISBN: 978-1-9822-4821-5 (e)

Balboa Press rev. date: 05/22/2020

ABOUT THE AUTHOR

David Lariviere has been a writer and editor for four decades. He was a sports editor at two New Jersey daily newspapers and has worked at companies such as CNBC, Dow Jones, the New York Post, the New York Daily News, the Star-Ledger and the Educational Testing Service. He covered the New York Mets' 1986 World Series championship season.

FOREWORD

The year 2020 will unfortunately be looked back upon by historians as the Year of the Coronavirus. As of this writing, we are just beginning to feel its tragic effect on our lives in the United States and throughout the world. Like no other news event in my lifetime, it has invaded our personal space tremendously. The massive unemployment, the closure of restaurants and schools and the stay-at-home orders cannot be ignored. Everyone has to pay some attention to the news to receive the latest information.

This book is a poignant, funny and practical survival guide on how to cope with the isolation-at-home aspect of this crisis. While nothing about people being sick and dying is humorous of course, we all need distractions so we don't lose our minds. This book provides tips and advice on productive ways to spend your time, rather than wasting it. No one wants to wake up one day in August and say, "Gee, if only I had done something useful with those four months I was stuck at home."

The tips are divided into four categories: helping others, self-improvement, home improvement and entertainment. Obviously not every tip will apply to everyone. But my hope is there are a few here that apply to you and your family – and some that apply to everybody.

I would like to dedicate this project to all those who sadly lost their lives to this virus and their loved ones. I would also like to thank my contributor and editor Paul Franklin, designer Craig Zavetz, Andrea Kane, Robert Schott, Rachel Hamilton and, last but certainly not least, my loving wife, Laura, for their support and inspiration.

Photo by Sean Kane

HELPING OTHERS

1

Do something nice for a health-care worker you know. They are our army on the front lines in this war and deserve to be revered just as much as a soldier in the jungle for putting their lives at risk to save ours. One of the first deaths reported was a Chinese doctor who had tried to warn the government but was ignored. We can't make the same mistake. Send a doctor or nurse you know who is in the fight a care package of food, a bouquet of beautiful flowers, or just a card or a note to tell them you are thinking about them and appreciate their daily sacrifices. I know it would mean the world to them and it should make you feel great as well!

2

Support your community and local restaurants by ordering takeout and delivering food to neighbors and needy people. Going out to get pizza, Chinese, Mexican food or whatever you like is a way to get out of the house and help these suffering businesses during a difficult time. By delivering it to elderly neighbors, you are doubling down on the impact you're making in your town. When you go, you might want to add a nice tip if you are able to. Hopefully, the federal relief bill keeps these places solvent until they can re-open for seating in the coming months. Maybe when people do go back, they'll actually sit and talk to each other, rather than spend time on cell phones, a real pet peeve of mine.

3

Make a pledge to volunteer your time for those less fortunate. Depending on where you live, this may not be able to be done until stay-at-home orders have been lifted. However, this crisis is sure to have far-reaching effects on the homeless, elderly, the disabled and the poor. Vow to yourself you will create time in your busy schedule, even if it's once a month, to work at a soup kitchen serving meals or something else to help people in your community or a neighboring one. Many activities like these are organized by churches so can coincide with your faith but you don't need an organization to get involved. These selfless acts will surely do wonders for the people you help and make you feel good when you look in the mirror as well.

4

Commit to working on a major political campaign. We have a presidential election plus all the Congressional contests in November and it's the perfect opportunity to get involved no matter whom you support. You'll meet a lot of passionate people of different ages and persuasions and, as you unite behind a common cause, you will have an opportunity to influence others. This can take many forms: you could get on a phone bank, attend rallies (assuming those restrictions are lifted by then) or canvass door to door. Regardless of the state of the coronavirus, you can bet the elections will still be held and you can make a difference in your community, your state and your country!

5

Make a phone call to someone you haven't talked to in a while. This would be particularly special if it's to someone you don't communicate with much or at all through text, email or social media. When I was younger, I could spend all day on the phone because of either my job as a journalist or talking to girlfriends (usually one at a time) or friends and family. My ear would hurt sometime, I was on the phone so long. But that is frowned upon now, like you're invading someone's personal space. How dare you call me on the phone? Why didn't you just text me, man? Most likely, that person will be thrilled to hear from you and will talk your ear off for an hour. Society has changed – we don't talk to people on the phone for 15 minutes, let alone an entire hour. And, because of the advances in technology, we've lost something. Something pretty special. Hearing someone's hearty laugh instead of seeing them type "LOL." It would be nice to get a little of that back.

6

Donate to a charity fighting the coronavirus. This one came up last year when both my parents died; my Mom in February from Alzheimer's and my Dad in September from congestive heart failure. I posted about both on Facebook and a donate button instantly popped up to battle these awful afflictions. Post about donating to a specific charity or even to give blood on your social media with a target goal you are seeking. In most cases, the money goes directly to the cause. Another feel-good opportunity.

7

Collect old clothes you don't wear anymore and donate them. I've heard that a rule of thumb is, if you haven't worn something for a year, toss it. There are so many non-profit organizations such as The Salvation Army, numerous veterans groups and your local Goodwill that will happily take items and even pick them up. They especially like shoes I'm told. My brother and I brought countless numbers of bags to Goodwill when emptying my parents' house. Many of the employees are vets or disabled so you are helping them at the same time. You can also donate books, records, games, toys, DVDs and furniture as well.

8

Write silly notes or a diary/life story and deliver them to nursing home patients. Our loved ones in nursing homes are scared and alone as visitation has been cut off. Receiving notes and words of encouragement will do wonders for their morale and, who knows, maybe literally save their lives. Many of the facilities often have entertainers come to sing and enlighten them. That is not happening now. Any kind of contact from the outside world will be most welcome to them. P.F.

9

Educate your kids and friends on the coronavirus. Obviously, we are inundated by the media every day on what we should be doing during this pandemic but it doesn't hurt to be on top of it yourself. Knowing the symptoms is the top priority as well as washing your hands thoroughly 10 to 15 times a day. Learn what the terms such as "shelter in place," "quarantine," "flattening the curve," "social distancing," and "PPE" (personal protective equipment) mean. Be aware of what stores are open in your area and which are considered "nonessential." Make sure you have received your relief check from the government if you're eligible. Also, file for unemployment benefits if applicable. It's not a good time to be uninformed.

10

Inspire others to appreciate government officials and the media. This is more in the category of the common good but the leadership some of our public officials have shown, particularly New York Gov. Andrew Cuomo, has been extraordinary. As a society, we are so quick to criticize politicians for either doing nothing or taking money away from us but, in this time of crisis, we are seeing their true colors and why they are needed. As far as the media, I am biased but I would argue it has done a marvelous job of doing its job – keeping us informed. There certainly is no shortage of news on the coronavirus and it can be too much for me at times but I have to say that it's comforting to know it – and our government – is there for us.

11

Register people to vote. In line with trying to do something good for your fellow countrymen, how about doing your civic duty by registering people to vote who haven't been for whatever reason? We still have no idea what effect the virus and the social distancing steps taken might have on the election on Nov. 3. But it gives us with free time plenty of opportunities to use it for good. Talk to the people in your family and your neighborhood and ask them if they're registered. If not, figure out how to change that. If they are older, offer to drive them to the polls assuming elections are held as usual. If it's changed to a mail vote, get their addresses and phone numbers so you can remind them to vote as the Big Day nears. This is a nonpartisan issue – you don't care if they're Democrats, Republicans or independents – get them to vote! Collectively, it will make a huge difference in our political process and fill a void that's been missing for a long time.

SELF-IMPROVEMENT

12

Have coronavirus-free media days. Here's one that is tough for me to propose to you because I love news and new information so much. But I recommend that you force yourself to have some "coronavirus-free" days. By that I mean, you don't watch or listen to any news at all that would be providing the latest updates of cases, deaths, etc. ... If you're on the Internet or phone, try not to look at the headlines and do not click on any stories about the virus. How often you can do that may depend on your job or your life situation. But I would say a rule of thumb would be one day a week (for me it would be Saturday or Sunday.) I wouldn't advise doing it more than that because there is valuable information disseminated every day like a three-month delay in filing federal income taxes for example. However, you might just do it every other week if you don't feel like you have to be tuned in that much. I know I would find it very difficult to not learn about what's going on at least once per day!

13

Make sure you laugh every day. One of the things the late great college basketball coach Jim Valvano used to say is "you need to laugh every day." I would argue at least five times a day. So be obsessive about making that happen. Watch an old George Carlin HBO special or the comedian of your choice. Binge watch "Get Smart" or "Seinfeld," whatever is your pleasure. Come up with your own jokes if you can. Try to make sure you are with others while sharing these laughs because it will heighten the joyful experience. In this time of social isolation, we still need human interaction and laughing together is about as good as it gets. I think my wife married me because I could make her laugh – it certainly wasn't for my looks!

14

Improve your mental health. Many people will use this time off (hopefully) to get in better physical shape although staying at home, eating and vegging on the couch will be the norm for some. Obviously, going out for a walk every day is a great idea. But, even maybe more important, is doing something to improve your mental health, something most of us ignore. I'll be honest enough to admit I've been to therapy in my life and it helps as long as you are seeing someone who is competent. Psychiatrists are still seeing patients online through this crisis. The financial burdens people will endure because of being out of work is depressing and people need to address that immediately. Don't let it linger too long!

15

Dream, dream, dream. I don't know about you but I'm a daydreamer. I can sit on my couch in the den at night for three hours and just stare at the walls, alone with my thoughts. It's some of the most enjoyable time that I spend (I hope my wife Laura doesn't read this part!) That's how I came up with the bright idea of sharing these tips with you! So carve out an hour of time in your day. It can be early in the morning after a workout or late at night before going to sleep. And just let your mind wander to anywhere it wants to travel. Think about work and how you can manage the next day. Think about an opportunity missed in the past that you would change if you could. Think about loved ones who have passed. Or think about something you could do in the future that would be unique to you. Something nobody could do but you. And think about how you could make that dream happen.

16

Surprise your wife with a home-cooked meal. Most men, especially married ones, have no clue about how to cook. In addition to losing my parents last year, we also lost Laura's surrogate mother, Sondra,.suddenly last summer. Although 93, she was sharp as a whip and tough as nails and not afraid to speak her mind. She loved us both dearly and we would visit her often to eat dinner and listen to live music by a terrific singer and piano player by the name of Fred Miller. One of her favorite rants to me (in a nice way sort of) was that I should learn how to cook. So, in a tribute to her, I really ought to. It's not too difficult as these days you can find all kinds of recipes online. So hit the grocery store and then shock your wife by making her dinner! You never know – it might become a regular thing.

17

Get smart about your finances and investments. This is important at any age but particularly if you're young. It's something that isn't taught in school (although it should be) but knowledge most people rely on an adviser for or learn on their own. But, even if you have a great adviser, you should know at least the basics yourself. It's similar to having a super mechanic for your car but being able to fix it yourself in a pinch. I remember when I started working, I got a subscription to Money magazine and taught myself about mutual funds. Soon, I was investing the extra money from my paycheck and getting a good return. The stock market is an extremely volatile place to be right now but wise investments will make you a lot of money in the long run.

18

Bring structure to your day. With so much free time now, it's easy to lose your focus. I saw a post by actor Mark Wahlberg once where he had everything in his day scripted to the minute, including meals and sleep. I don't advocate that necessarily but some structure is needed so you don't waste time. Plan a certain time for your workout and daily walk. If you're not working, there needs to be an allocated time for job searching and, maybe more importantly, thinking about what you want to do specifically rather than blindly responding to ads. Make time for family and entertainment, hopefully combined but also separately. Take a nap for an hour or two. It should give you a boost to make it through the day rather than relying on caffeine.

19

Think about how you can augment your looks. Here's one focusing on vanity, specifically your looks. Most of us gaze at the mirror in the morning every day when we're getting ready for work and don't think twice about the face we see. But now that you're home all the time, it's time to take a closer peak. Is it time to shave off that beard or mustache? (Especially for the women!) Maybe think about new glasses or contacts if you have glasses. How about a new hairstyle for when hair salons open again? Lose that 20-30 pounds you've been meaning to shed. Sorry, no elective surgery is allowed but you can think about it now at least. How about turning that gray hair brown again? Our looks obviously affect the way we feel about ourselves so now's the time to take stock in you!

20

Think about not "social distancing" when you return to work. We're staying six feet apart from each other now but it's not a behavior we should get used to. It's obviously not normal. However, so many of us were/are trapped in extremely antisocial work settings, isolated in offices and cubicles. We eat lunch by ourselves and rarely interact with our co-workers. Some departments, although small, are so unfriendly that you're lucky if you physically see your supervisor more than twice a week. Vow that when you return to work that you will change – that you'll make time for lunch with colleagues, that you'll visit people to chat – even if it's not work-related – rather than just emailing or texting all day. By the end of this crisis, we all should be starved for human interaction. Don't shy away from it again when it's back!

21

Take stock of your faith or philosophy in life. Another powerful part of the human experience is faith or philosophy – your sense of your true purpose on the planet and, ultimately, what happens to you when you leave it. I was raised a strict Roman Catholic by very religious parents but strayed quickly after breaking my ankle while playing basketball in high school. I never really went back to church again after that – and I'm not sure my late parents ever truly forgave me. Now, I'm agnostic at best, an atheist at worst, as I wonder how a loving God could watch all the misery that takes place in this world to occur. I think of the death of a former colleague's young teenager due to cancer. How is that allowed to happen? Where ever you are in your journey of faith, take this extra time to re-examine it.

22

Solve crossword puzzles. Keeping the brain active is critical especially as we get older. One of the best ways to do that is to solve crossword puzzles although maybe stay away from The New York Times' ones. Buy a book of crosswords and attempt to do at least one per day. If you have not done them previously, it will be a struggle at first but, once you realize the consistencies of them and how many clues are repeated from one puzzle to another, you'll get better and be hooked. You'll be amazed at how much you increase your vocabulary and your reading ability while having fun!

23

Share a passion of yours with your partner. When I first got married to Laura, she introduced me to a world I had never known before – fashion. She had InStyle magazines larger than my phone book. I was told these were the fall fashion preview editions. Before I knew it, I was watching Isaac Mizrahi shows on QVC ("Are you kidding me?", "Gorgeous!") and learning about peplum and reversible watches. I didn't mind at all. Now, we watch them together weekly. I wouldn't have been caught dead doing that 20 years earlier! My suggestion is for spouses to pick a strong interest of each other's and spend time with them learning about it and why they love it so much. Get to enjoy it with them and be somewhat knowledgeable about it and it will make the bond you have together even stronger! Staying at home doesn't have to be about isolation; it can be about sharing and growing together.

24

Have "cell phone free" days. Someone I used to work with who is as unique as they come often tells me she can't wait until she retires so she can "get rid of her smartphone forever." I'm as addicted to my phone as anyone, texting friends and family and checking my email and social media hourly it seems whether I'm at work or at home. I propose days when we turn our phones off and put them in a drawer somewhere and leave them there. Like a drug, it would be so tempting to open the drawer and check it – but you can't! Now I realize there are emergencies that could come up – so give your loved ones a heads-up when you're doing this so they can contact you in other ways. How often you choose to do this is up to you but try it let's say twice a month and see how it feels.

25

Force yourself to read more. Being stuck at home doesn't mean you have to watch TV all day. Carve out time for listening to music and reading books, magazines and newspapers. Are they still around? Clicking on Internet links is one thing but try to do it the old-fashioned way – with the physical book in your hand. Set goals for how many chapters or pages you want to get through in one day and when you want to have a book finished. My late father used to read more than 200 books a year. No joke. He kept a list of what he read. (Maybe that's how I developed my fetish for lists).

26

Learn something new involving technology. Maybe about downloading apps on to your phone. It's something I've never done. Sharpen your skills on Microsoft Word, Excel and Power Point. Play around with your phone to maximize its use. There are so many different functions to these smartphones that most of us are unaware of and never use.

27

If you are of a certain age, consider retiring. It's probably best to talk to a financial adviser first but this may be the perfect opportunity to move on with your life now that you're home and getting used to being away from the workplace. If you decide to retire, first make sure you have a plan on something constructive you want to do with the rest of your life. Write that book you were always thinking about. Go to those cities or countries you've always wanted to visit. New Orleans and San Francisco would top my list. Remember, use this time to reflect about everything and retiring may be a great option for you now.

28

Mend rifts with family and friends. Many of us are estranged from members of our family over stupid disputes that just grew out of proportion over the years. To not be speaking to brothers and sisters is just not right. Take the extra time to try to mend the fences with these family members. Social media has also caused dumb squabbles between friends who used to be extremely close. Reach out to these people. Take the initiative yourself. Lose that pride and make the first move. Don't be stubborn. You'll be glad you did!

29

Create something artistic. Now, mind you, this is coming from a kid who couldn't even color within the lines and was scared to death whenever I was given a class assignment requiring artistic talent. Help, Mom! But this is a great time to get some paint and put something on an easel (try not to do this in the living room because your wife might get angry!). Or just sketch something on a pad. Remember, let your mind wander and use your imagination. Draw a person you admire like an athlete or actor. Look outside your window and sketch the nature and the houses. Whatever strikes your fancy. It will be liberating for you!

30

Research colleges. If you have kids in high school or even younger, you might want to use this time to thoroughly research colleges. It is one of the most important decisions anyone ever makes but I know I for one didn't take it seriously. I wanted to study communications and I knew Syracuse University was one of the best in the country so I applied and got in. I think I may have applied to two other places – but didn't visit any. I'm not saying choosing Syracuse was a mistake but, in hindsight, I would have done a lot more research before making a selection. There are now companies that will help you match your child to the specific college that suits them best academically, socially and geographically. A friend of mine has actually started one in New Jersey called Admissions on Track.

31

Do a "Where do I want to be in six months?" exercise. OK, a project about perspective and goals. Picture yourself three, six or 12 months from now, whenever this crisis is over and we can resume our normal lives. What do you want to accomplish in that time? If you write a plan along with specific actionable steps to achieve it, you have a much better chance to make it a reality. These aren't like New Year's resolutions like losing weight or exercising more. This is a total picture of where you want to be in your life compared to where you are now. For example, if you're not working, target a company where you want to work, research them thoroughly, find some names of employees and be ready to execute a full-out assault on them when this crisis ends where you can sell yourself to fit a need they have. If you are working, think about your place in the company and where you want to go and how you're going to get there when people stop working remotely. You'll be way ahead of your co-workers if you do.

32

Learn how to make your own food and alcohol. If you've got a green thumb, now's the time to cultivate that garden you've always wanted to grow. Tomatoes, corn, cucumbers, carrots, beans, and whatever else you like. It will save on trips and expenses at the crowded grocery store for one. Another idea is to try to brew your own beer. My brother-in-law has done this I know. I get the idea it's kind of like being a mad scientist in a lab, that it's a lot of trial and error before you make one that tastes just right. But that's the fun part — and you have the time so why not?

33

Write your own obituary. This may seem kind of maudlin but it's actually a good exercise in reflection and potentially self-improvement. I must advise that you should be honest in doing this. But think back on your life and how you will most likely be remembered. For example, mine might start something like this: "David Lariviere, a New Jersey journalist, sports editor and author for more than 60 years (I wish) passed away yesterday in his sleep at his home in Lawenceville at the age of 95. He leaves behind his 27-year-old wife Laura (just kidding and another I wish)." LOL! It forces you to look back at what you have accomplished (or sadly not accomplished) and what you want to do before you die.

34

Reminisce with someone about good times you shared. The best way to do this is in-person but a phone call, text or chat on social media is the next best thing. I am someone who thinks about the past all the time – too much for my own good really. But it doesn't get any better than sharing a conversation and a laugh or two about a night at work 25 years ago that was either really tense or silly. All our lives and associations have changed so much but what we have in common is our shared memories. Recapturing them at a reunion or on the phone is so special and fulfilling. We all could use that so desperately right now.

35

Write down your dreams. I often have extremely visual dreams at night but, minutes after I wake up, I can't remember any of them. So keep a note pad by your bed and, if you arise in the middle of the night, write down what you were dreaming in as much detail as you can. When you wake up, do the same. Tell your spouse what you dreamed and talk about it to see if you can make sense of it. If you are in therapy, bring the pad to your doctor and ask them what they mean. Maybe you'll discover something about yourself you didn't know that can help you cope more with your daily life.

36

Have a baby! Probably the best way to improve yourself and your family is to add to it especially with both of you at home constantly now. In nine months, when this crisis is hopefully over, you will really have something awesome to show for the time. Just don't name him or her "Corona" or "Covid." Probably not a great idea.

37

Write or revise your will. This isn't to say you're going to die any time soon but it's a good time to take stock of your assets and how you want to allocate them to your children upon your passing. You will need to get a good attorney as I would not advise doing this online. It's another way to give yourself more peace of mind during a distressing period in our lives.

38

Create a swear jar in your house. How many of us could benefit by cleaning up our language? One way to do that is to enact monetary penalties for profanity. If someone utters the F word, they have to donate say a dollar to the jar. See how much it grows by the end of a week and use the proceeds for takeout or charity. You'll find you'll think twice about cursing before too long. When Laura and I first started dating, we had one for negative comments we said about each other. I always filled that one up. A great way to start a relationship, right? Well, she did wind up marrying me so it all worked out in the end!

39

Write about a place you've never visited. I thought of this one after listening to a recent LP called "Buried Treasure" by one of my favorite singers, Jimmy Buffett. Yes, I'm a parrothead! He said, in his early days as a songwriter, he wrote a tune about Paris although he had never actually been there. Imagination is a powerful tool we have as human beings but you need to stoke it and use it. So think of a city or place you have never visited and write about how you picture it, the sky, the landscape, the stores, everything. Let your mind wander and see what kind of picture you can paint. When we're allowed to travel again, go there and see if your mind's image was anywhere close to the reality.

40

Find a map and discover the world of geography. Since you didn't pay attention in elementary school, find a U.S. or world map and make up for that deficiency now. Take a blank map and see how many states and countries you can identify. Then do some studying and try again later. This could also serve as a planning guide for your cross country trip that you will appreciate more than ever once we are let out of this prison. P.F.

41

Be wary of scams trying to bilk you because of your vulnerability financially due to the virus. I get emails every day trying to get me to be a broker and purchaser for some company or to help someone with a pretty picture inherit a half million dollars in Ghana. Don't fall for them! I also was watching a show about deadly cults on the History Channel recently describing how so many people join cults and commit suicide. Remember the Jonestown Massacre and Heaven's Gate. Although isolated in our homes, we all have an innate sense of belonging and being with other people. Don't let your loneliness make you succumb to a cult-like group trying to take your money and your independence.

42

Write your own song or poem. I'm not talking about the music part but if you have that talent, go for it! I'm referring to the words. An easy way to do it is google an existing song and change the words to something else like I recently did, altering "My Sharona" to "Bye Corona" just for fun. Or you can start from scratch and write something original about love, family, home or maybe something people can sing while washing their hands 10 times a day! It's not as hard as it sounds, again, if you let your mind wander! Post what you write on your social media and get your friends' and family's reaction.

43

Conduct an imagination writing lesson for your kids. I'm not a teacher but I don't think we do enough to stimulate the creative minds of our children. Use this time at home as parents to change that! Ask your kids a thought-provoking question such as "Do you believe there is alien life on other planets?" and have them write an essay on why they think so, what it might look like, etc. ... You could always go with the standby, "Write about what you want to be when you grow up" but that's a little tired IMO. Think of something a bit out of the ordinary that may pertain to their particular interests. You want them to be as creative as they can. Give them a reasonable deadline depending on their age and writing ability and then read it with them. It will be a shared fun learning experience for the entire family!

44

Eliminate some of your vices like drugs, smoking and alcohol. This may be the hardest one on the list to execute. With more time on our hands than ever before, it's more likely that our smoking and drinking will increase rather than decline – but that's something to be wary of too. I don't know the latest statistics but let's not forget we had an opiod epidemic before this pandemic struck. It will still be around after COVID-19 leaves. Sometimes it's the people who can least afford to spend money on drugs, cigarettes and beer who lay out the cash for it. It's not a good way to use that federal relief check. The pressure on many of us right now is high so it's easy to puff on that cig, light up that joint or have that extra glass of chardonnay. But maybe it's also the time to stop – or wean yourself off at least.

45

Be prepared when your spouse/partner passes on. None of us really know when we're going to die but some of us get very sick before moving on. Try to be as mentally and emotionally ready as you can for the eventuality of losing your spouse. Don't leave things unsaid that you'll regret forever. If you have any secrets you want to divulge, now is the time. Make sure you know how to handle the finances if your spouse does them now or, most likely if you're a guy, be certain you can operate the washer/drawer and kitchen appliances so you don't go hungry. Have important phone numbers like relatives, hospitals, doctors, dentists, police, lawyer, etc. ... readily available.

46

Take the time and effort to get to know your neighbors. This is another exercise in being sociable. In the past, neighbors used to be friendly to each other. But that has also changed for the worse in the last few years. Growing up, I remember neighbors constantly visiting us and bringing baked goods too! Now, we barely make eye contact or say hello. Having good neighbors is important in times of need with the potential of social unrest. You want to know if someone's been parked in front of your house while you were at work all day. So I suggest you vow to open up the lines of communication with 4 to 5 neighbors, try to collect cell numbers and email addresses and stay in touch. They could be extremely valuable associations.

47

Try to broaden your political influences – at least for a day! Needless to say, the political divide in the country is as wide as the Grand Canyon. And that needs to change quickly (easy for me to say, right?). So, if you tend to lean to the left, spend a day where the only network you obtain your news is Fox. If you're on the right side of the ledger, no watching anything but MSNBC or CNN. It will be difficult to do – almost impossible at times – but stay disciplined. Reflect on how the day's stories were told and ask yourself if it had an effect at all on your viewpoint. Try to imagine what total inundation of watching news from this perspective would have on you. It may make no difference in your overall outlook but, hell, maybe it will. It's worth a shot.

48

Exercise with your spouse/partner and/or your kids. Most people get up early and go out for a run. Or go to the gym after work. We squeeze exercise in when convenient in our hectic schedules. Now that we're all at home together, there's no reason not to get in shape at the same time! By doing that, we can encourage each other and grow closer. Maybe even invite a neighbor every now and then.

49

Have a coin jar to throw your loose change in. When I was single, I had this huge jar from who knows where I got it. At the end of each day I began to toss my change into it. After several years, the container was nearly full so I secured some penny, nickel, dime and quarter rolls and started to fill them up. When I totaled all the rolls, it came to about $50 I wouldn't have had otherwise. I don't remember what I spent it on – probably some CDs – but that's not the point. We can all use as much cash on hand as we can amass these days.

50

If working from home, don't do as much as you would at the workplace. Remember, on the job, you would be mingling and chatting with co-workers, sitting in boring meetings where you wouldn't be paying attention, etc. ... Cut that time off your work day – that's yours for relaxing and spending more time with your family. I'm not saying to totally slough off but hard workers deserve a break these days. Take advantage of it. Don't make any employer abuse this time to make you work more than you would normally! (Of course, this is easy for me to say because I'm not working right now!).

HOME IMPROVEMENT

51

Spend more time cooking lavish, multi-course meals. Now that most everyone is working from home, now's your opportunity to spread your wings in the kitchen. Have a number of dishes on your stove simmering at the same time, maybe some broth, some veggies, or whatever. Try to make most meals healthy and delicious rather than just something you need to shove in your mouth while working at your desk. Maybe take a day and look through your pantry/cabinets and experiment by making an original meal. Pot luck if you will. Now, I'm the worst person you want preparing a meal as the only items I know how to make in a kitchen are ice cubes and toast but this tip should be great for the majority of you!

52

Organize your closets by color, season and category. This project, crafted by Laura of course, could take a day, a week, or months. But once finished, it can be a work of art! And you'll have more fun to get dressed and accessorize – when we're allowed to leave our homes again of course in 2021! Start by separating clothing into categories: tops, sweaters, jeans, pants, skirts, dresses, blazers, suits, jackets and, finally, coats. You can color coordinate how ever you like, for example, blues together, then reds, pinks, and whites. Blacks together, then greys, golds, beiges, off whites. Greens together, then turquoise, limes and yellows. Purples, then lavenders, lilacs, and so forth. Then put spring and summer outfits together. In order, go with light sweaters, then tops, jeans. The fall/winter side can be arranged in the same way. Depending on how many closets you have, one closet could be red, white and blue and another could be blacks, greys and purples. Then one of greens and yellows, etc. ... The trick is to try to keep it seasonal and have like colors together, so it's easy to see your options for your outfit coordination. L.L.

53

Shred old papers. In cleaning out your closets and drawers, take those documents from long ago – legal bills, car bills, college bills, divorce papers (things you have horded for absolutely no reason) ... and shred them. It will make you feel a whole lot better. When I was cleaning out my parents' house after they passed away last year, I found old high school newspapers with my articles, which were fun to read to see how terrible a writer I was back then – but not necessary to keep. No shredder for them – just the garbage can. P.F.

54

Adopt a pet. Pet stores are still open so it's a perfect time to add a dog or cat to the family especially now that you're home to take care of it. I'm partial to cats myself but dogs give you an opportunity to get outside and walk them every day. The love of a pet will help the pain of isolation especially if you live by yourself. But it's also an awesome gift to your kids as you can teach them the responsibility of caring for someone other than themselves. The naming of a pet is also a fun family exercise. The only down side is they do get sick and die which can be devastating. But the positives of the love they give outweigh their eventual loss.

55

Make your own clothes. If you can knit or crochet, now's the time to reap what you sew! A lot of retail clothing stores are closed so why not make your own if you can? I was thinking mostly for your children but it could be for yourself or anyone, even your pets, probably the dog more than the cat though. It takes time (I'm told) but would save money and spike your creativity.

56

Rearrange the furniture in your house. Maybe it's time for a new point of view – even from home. Rearrange the pictures on the wall. In the bedroom, move the bed from its current position to a new one. Have the bed face the window, place it on an angle between two walls, or just relocate it. Then put the other furniture pieces in new spots as well. In the living room or dining room also move big pieces first. The couch can face in a new position and then relocate the chairs, tables, etc. ... to a new area. Then if your rooms have a neutral base color like gray, beige, white, black, brown, tan, you can switch out the accent color you now have like purple or lavender to say green and/or yellow. Order silk flowers, throw pillows, vases, or different decor in that new color to further change the space. These new looks may be just the lift you need to feel like you are someplace new! L.L.

57

Make a home inventory video for insurance purposes. Now's the opportunity to do it while you're home before a fire, flood or other unforeseen natural disaster hits! Walk through your house, your garage, your attic, basement, etc. ... and talk about your possessions of value, how much they are worth and their age. Make sure you also know where everything is as well in addition to your birth certificate, social security card, passport, etc. ... Again, this isn't something most of us normally do during the hustle and bustle of our daily lives. Doing it now makes a lot of sense.

58

Go through and clean out your medicine cabinet. It's a great time to scan your medications, lotions, potions, creams, ointments, sprays and healers to see if they're expired or been on the shelf too long. Throw away anything that's out of date. Decide what you need to replace and make a list. Order or shop for new updated versions of what you have discarded. It's also a good time to check first aid supplies like band aids of different sizes, gauze. tape, something for burns and bruises, and an antibiotic ointment. Make sure you have ice packs in the freezer, mouthwash or sore throat spray, and fresh toothpaste, brushes and floss. Remember S-tay safe, O-rganize health supplies, A-dd new items and P-repare to take care of yourself! L.L.

ENTERTAINMENT

59

Take a ride into the country, especially this time of the year. Bring your camera or cell phone and take shots of not only nature, but say old barns, whatever. You could make them into a large flip calendar and give for special occasion presents. In this time of self-isolation, it is important to get outside every day to get a breath of fresh air and stay sane. I would suggest making it a geographic exercise as well by taking a map of your state and picking a spot where you have never been to drive to. Or check out a town or county you are considering to relocate to in the future. P.F.

60

Write a love letter to your spouse or partner. This was a suggestion by Laura as we just celebrated our 10th wedding anniversary. Obviously being the lifetime writer that I am, I advocate writing as much as you can. It's become a lost art in the world like bunting in baseball and a skill not appreciated as much as others like those of doctors, lawyers or even accountants. Ugh! Many of us old fogies used to write love letters to our girlfriends and boyfriends when separated by a distance at college. It was too expensive then to talk much on the phone and, believe it or not, there were no computers or cell phones back then. (Yes, I am old!). Sitting down at a desk and writing a love letter to your girl/guy was a great way to think of them fondly and communicate your loving thoughts to them even though they weren't there with you. Sometimes, they got really mushy too! So bring back that old exercise and write a love letter to your spouse. It will rekindle your relationship.

61

Stick to the positives of social media. There are a lot of negative consequences about Facebook but try to take advantage of the good aspects of it during this down time. One of those is finding and re-connecting with high school and college classmates, something I have been able to do in the 11 years I've been on Facebook. I have built many close relationships that I didn't have before and maintained others that might have been lost otherwise. That has resulted in reunions that have been special, both in high school, and in small gatherings of my fraternity brothers. We wish each other Happy Birthday, and try to check in as much as possible. I was greatly comforted after I lost my parents last year by the words of high school friends, a couple of whom were even nice enough to attend the wakes and funerals. Support systems are crucial and social media used correctly can be one of the best we have today.

62

Create Final Four frustration brackets. Choose your field of 68 teams. Then take a pack of playing cards. To simulate the games, change the format from two halves to four quarters. Each team draws two cards for each quarter. Face cards are worth 10 points while every other card is worth its number value. For example, if you draw a five of diamonds and a jack of spades, that's 15 points. Play until four quarters are completed or even overtime. Advance the winning team in the bracket. At halftime or in between games, grab a cold Corona beer from the fridge! P.F.

63

Binge-watch TV series. This is my suggestion for you. Divide them into categories: ones you can watch with your kids, those you can view with your wife or husband and those you would like to take in on your own. I would further categorize them (remember I have OCD!) into new and old shows. I'm a science fiction freak so get me all the old episodes of "The X-Files," Rod Serling's "The Twilight Zone," and "Star Trek," and I'll be happy as a clam for a couple of months. My wife likes police and murder shows like "Law and Order," "Columbo" and "Perry Mason." As far as new offerings, I would suggest going out of your element and trying a genre you don't normally watch. If you don't enjoy it, you can always ditch it and go to something else. Don't feel obligated to continue. Maybe this is the time to get that Netflix subscription as well.

64

Have family game nights. When I was growing up, I was a board game nerd. Monopoly, Scrabble, Parcheesi, Risk, Chutes and Ladders, you name it, we had it and we played it, often as a family. Being the spoiled brat that I was, I was very competitive and didn't like to lose so, many times upon the moment of defeat, I would lose my temper, scatter the pieces on the board and demand that my siblings play with me again until I won. Sometimes they did. Sometimes they didn't. So plan a regular game night with your family, or even play cards if that's all you have. It should be fun and, remember, it doesn't matter if you win or lose! Don't be a brat like I was!

65

Play mind games with your spouse. Well, maybe that came out wrong. When Laura and I were first dating, we used to play this game in bed. (Watch it, dirty minds!). Laura called it "Person, Place or Thing." One person has to think of a person, place or thing, often pertaining to something that happened or was discussed during our time together that day. For example, an actor in a movie we saw, a place we talked about visiting or an object (that was always the toughest one!). The other person has to ask questions to determine what that person, place or thing is like, "Is the person on TV?", "Is it a place in New Jersey," or "Is it a thing located in our house?" The faster you guess it correctly, the more points you score. Play as many rounds as you want. Try it. It's fun.

66

Spend an afternoon going through old collections. Whether it be coins, stamps, baseball cards, programs from games attended, tickets from concerts or knicknacks you have no idea where they come from -- relive some old memories. I reluctantly had to throw out many items like these when cleaning out my parents' house. Many of us are hoarders but the reason I think is because we want to hold on to good memories as long as we can. That day you saw Mantle hit one out at the old Yankee Stadium. The tickets to that Lynryd Skynrd show you saw just before their plane crashed. That program you kept when your Dad taught you how to keep score for the first time. Awards and trophies could also be included here. Life is not just about living for the present and the future but remembering the good parts of your past as well.

67

Play outdoor games with your kids. The old staples of hide and seek, scavenger hunt and capture the flag are three that come to mind. Hide baseballs, candy, pictures, coins, whatever you choose. When I was a kid, I had a huge backyard and woods in the back I would walk in constantly. My best friend lived on the other side of the woods so it was an adventure every day I went to play with him.

68

Discover the world of talk radio. Many of us listen to sports radio in the car but, with no sports going on any longer, how about getting turned on by National Public Radio (NPR)? It's informative, funny, and thought-provoking. There are also plenty of political shows, mostly catering to the far right, to get into. Again, something you didn't have time to do before.

69

Have more sex! Yeah, you read that right. We're all couped up in many stay-at-home ordered states. We're either working from home or out of work. I can only watch so much TV in any one day. Naps, as I have said, are enjoyable. Why not take them together with your partner? Showering together is also suggested. It's a clean way to be dirty. Look at how much money you would save on your water bill! Try to be more creative in bed with your partner. Try things you have not attempted before. Maybe watch some porn together? Remember, this is all about having fun!

70

Alphabetize your music collection. So I'm obsessive-compulsive about my belongings. What would be a blast for me would be to gather all of my records and CDs into two piles. I would then put them in alphabetical order. (My large Beatles' collection would go under "B" while my Bruce Springsteen stack would fall under "S.") I would then put a record on (Aerosmith possibly) and listen to it all the way through. Then I would take the first CD off my pile (maybe

ABBA, ha!) and play that. And so on until I was done. For a music nut like me, this exercise would take up several months and, of course, could be completed while working on other things. Estimate how long it would take for you and see how close your estimate comes to the actual amount of listening time.

71

If you're single, explore the world of online, visual dating. I'm not sure what young high school and college kids are doing for dates now because movie theaters, bars, plays, sports, concerts and restaurants are shuttered. Are parents even allowing their kids to see their sweethearts? I would think so. But, it's certainly not the best time to meet someone if you're unattached at any age. I've heard that some people are connecting through various online dating services where they chat and see each other over the computer. It's a great way to get to know someone and, for guys, you don't have to pick up the check. It also eliminates that awkward do I kiss her or not moment when you both go home. Of course, there are disadvantages too as I'm sure you can imagine.

72

Have fun with Google. Because I get bored very easily and am often up daydreaming late at night while everyone else is asleep, I sometimes find myself googling people from my past. So here's your task: think of a job you've had from a few years ago -- the people you worked with, your bosses, your staff, people you liked to talk to and the people who you gritted your teeth with and tried to avoid. The guy in a cubicle who would make a racket while eating lunch at his desk for example. Bling! Bang! Bong! Boom! What, are you eating or trying to kill bugs? Google as many as you want, say 5 to 10, and try to determine where they're working now, what their position is (Are they a cushy vice president at a major bank?) and if they are still alive in some cases. Once you have found everyone you want, consider contacting them through email or social media if appropriate to catch up or network. It may lead to a productive job opportunity. You have nothing to lose!

73

Find those old books that were gifts that you never read. I have hard-cover books about trains, pirates, the Grand Canyon and touring MLB ballparks. I also have self-help books, books to get in shape, historical books, books on writing (which I should have read before starting this project), sports books, music books and coffee table books. (Unfortunately, I don't have a coffee table so they are stacked in the garage!). P.F.

74

Broaden your alcohol taste. I have heard that business at the liquor stores is brisk. (I'm not a big drinker anymore.) Wine sales, in particular, are up. So, why not use this time as an opportunity to diversify. Every week, try a wine you have not tasted before. If you're a beer drinker, go with a different IPA. You say you prefer hard liquor? If you're a Jack Daniels guy or gal, switch to gin for a week. Like your Scotch on the rocks? Buy some Petrone tequila. Literally, mix it up — maybe not on the same night though!

75

Choose a friend, male or female, and create a "pen pal." (Some people like me may have more trouble than others finding friends but I can't help you there.) Communicate either through email or via old fashioned letter on a weekly basis. Can be actual information about what's going on in your life or complete fantasy. Pretend to be 10 years old (not hard for me), in high school or a parent of triplets. I think fantasy would be more fun and humorous. Maybe pretend to be friends who met at summer camp. P.F.

76

Play all your music by artist. Another exercise you can only do if you own a lot of CDs and /or records. If you're in a mood for a certain one of your artists, let's say the Eagles, play every one of their albums in the order they were recorded until you are finished. Then choose another artist of a different style, say AC/DC, and do the same. What I find when I do this is I gain a stronger appreciation for their music and it makes me want to fill in the gaps and buy the recordings I don't have by them. (Probably not a good idea if you're low on cash right now!).

77

Join a fan site. I'm a longtime New York Yankees fan myself and belong to one of these where there are daily posts, news, questions, old pictures, lists and discussions. Like name your favorite Yankee of all time by position or your top 10 all-time favorite players. There are fan sites for musicians, actors, comedians, politicians, college teams and I'm sure a lot more. Most of us don't have much time in our daily lives for these sites but many of us do now. Just be careful in terms of avoiding getting into heated arguments on these. It's not worth the agitation and chances are you'll probably be asked to leave. (It happened to a friend of mine not me of course!).

78

Investigate your family tree. This is something my late Aunt Lorraine did and that my cousin MaryAnn has continued. Check out your family tree on your father's and mother's sides to see how far it goes back and if you're related to anyone famous. There are many ways to do this but I'm told by a friend that Familysearch.org is free. In doing so, you can gather a lot of old pictures of relatives who died before you were born and maybe discover some cool stories about them too. It's about connecting with a link to your unique past that will tell you a little more about yourself now and maybe your future also.

79

Discover the world of podcasts. They are the new rage and range from the humorous to the political. I was listening to one recently by author Fran Leibowitz, who talked about how she doesn't own a cell phone. A friend asked her how she would know if someone is running late that she is meeting. The humorist snapped, "Well, they're not here, are they?" If you are so inclined, you might want to start a podcast yourself to see if you can get a following.

80

Go through your cable channel guide and pick one you have never watched. Watch it for a day, let's say. I'm a big History Channel guy myself as well as AMC. My wife likes Turner Classic Movies and QVC. Maybe it's CNBC or Bloomberg to become more knowledgeable about the stock market and finances. Maybe it's the Discovery Channel, HGTV or the Food Network to learn how to cook better meals. You may find you get hooked on it and it becomes a part of your regular viewing. Or not. If not, try another station until you find one that clicks.

81

Entertain your friends on social media such as Facebook with clever posts. For the past two years, I have compiled weekly music top 10 lists coalescing around a common theme. For example, I put together a 15-song "Coronavirus" list with titles such as "All Revved Up With No Place To Go" by Meat Loaf, "I Can't Get Next To You" by the Temptations and "Keep Your Hands to Yourself" by the Georgia Satellites. I reveal a song or two every day with the No. 1 song being posted on Sunday. I invite my friends to make their own nominations and often substitute their nods for those that I had chosen. It makes for a communal experience as people make comments on others' selections and mine. It's all for fun and laughs and the music. I usually listen to the songs I pick during the week I'm featuring them.

82

Play sports outside with your kids. It's the perfect time to put that hoop on your garage and develop that jump shot or improve your dribbling. Like I said, we had a huge backyard growing up and I can remember playing badminton with my late Dad and throwing baseballs, footballs and frisbees around. We also played croquet, a great lawn game, and hopscotch on the sidewalk with chalk and stones. Maybe you have horseshoes or a shuffleboard setup. Go through your garage and, while cleaning it, pull out those old games you haven't played in decades. Another great way to get in shape obviously!

83

Convert your old VCR tapes. Are any of you kids old enough to remember VCRs, otherwise known as videocassette recorders? They were the rage in the '80's before DVDs and DVR. Back to cleaning out my parents' house, I found a case of old VCR tapes I had, some that I had bought but many that I had made myself by recording movies, games, shows or concerts. Now I've been told there's a process to convert these old VCRs to DVDs through WalMart or the mail. I don't think it's cheap to do but if you have your wedding, home movies of when your kids were young or playing sports or music, it might be worth it to get them converted now.

84

Create your own system for tracking the top songs of the year. By now, you should realize I was a strange child. But, although I was the oldest of four, I knew how to entertain myself. When I started enjoying pop music in the early '70's, I discovered Casey Kasem's legendary "American Top 40" which aired on Sunday mornings in the New York area. I religiously wrote down each tune and kept the lists in a bound notebook. At the end of the year, Casey would count down the Top 100 hits. In 1974, I came up with a way I thought would tell me in advance what the year's Top 100 would be. I assigned points to No. 1 (80), No. 2 (78), etc. … down to No. 40 (2 points) and totaled them every week. A top song would garner hundreds of points depending on how long it remained in the survey. At the end of '74, my top song was Barbra Streisand's "The Way We Were," which wound up to be the No. 1 on Casey's list as well. I was thrilled!

85

As a family, read and/or perform scenes from a popular play. Go online and find parts of a script of a play your family has always enjoyed. Assign roles to family members and practice reading your lines. Plan a day that you'll sit and act out the play. Have someone record it if possible. Probably best to choose one with a limited number of characters. Laura suggested "Peter Pan," "Cinderella," "Fiddler on the Roof," "Oklahoma" and "Camelot" to name a few. But, remember, it's all about having fun!

86

Turn your house into a golf course. Get out your putter, a yard stick, or a cane. Create holes by laying that beer mug or glass on its side. (Just make sure you finish the contents first!). You could simulate traps by placing random objects on the carpet, maybe require hitting a ball under the couch toward a hole, or through a small chair or end table. The course could spread from the living room to the dining room to the kitchen. Or set it up in the basement. Or you could just go out in the backyard and really strike the ball if you can. No golf courses open and no live golf on TV to watch. Whoa is me! P.F.

87

Spend a clear night outside to look at the stars. When I was a Boy Scout in my youth, we used to go on camping trips every month. We pitched tents, cooked our own food and sat around campfires gazing at the sky. I knew my constellations back then – the Big Dipper and the Little Dipper – and the North Star. So I suggest, once it gets warm, you put a tent in the backyard, and lay on the ground on your back and just identify as many stars as you can. It can be educational, romantic and just plain fun! It will clear your mind as well.

88

Create your own unique language. When I was growing up, I literally made up words like "gronc" and "fraze," assigned meaning to them and used them regularly in conversations with my parents and siblings. It was kind of like pig Latin or the Shirley Ellis tune "The Name Game" where you could change the first names of your friends back in the day. So maybe it would be a silly, fun exercise to create your own words and put them into daily use in your home. If you're so inclined, the next time you're in an elevator, invoke your new language while strangers are around and enjoy the bizarre looks you receive. I did that with a college roommate once. It was hysterical.

89

Take a video of your spouse or roommate singing a song. Use a fork or spoon for a microphone and let it fly shouting out the words and swinging your hips with no musical background. Pick a tune that is well-known and that people like such as Neil Diamond's "Sweet Caroline," Bruce Springsteen's "Glory Days" or Billy Joel's "New York State of Mind." Try to post it on your social media and wait for the ensuing laughter and insults (hopefully more of the former than the latter)! P.F.

90

Google the places where you used to live. A friend who resides in Idaho tells me that, on average, people move every three to five years. So employ Google Earth to locate all of your previous abodes and view what they look like now. Earlier this year, I sold my family's home that my late parents lived in for 52 years. I sold it to a group that will most likely demolish it – so it would be interesting to see what kind of house gets built in its place.

91

Take virtual tours of national parks and museums. In lieu of going on vacation, try to substitute for it by using your computer to take these trips. When this crisis is over, plan to actually travel to your favorite place. P.F.

92

Take a trip to the cemetery. Go visit that late family member you've been thinking about for years. Spend an hour or so reflecting on what that person meant to you and what they did to make you a better person. Try to honor their memory by being more like that person. P.F.

93

Have your kids keep a daily journal about their activities during this crisis. I have hopefully provided some thoughtful and useful tips for how to keep your children active and productive. And you know by now I want kids to write as much as they can. It doesn't have to be too involved but it could be a terrific keepsake for their children and grandchildren to read years from now.

94

Finish something that you started years ago. Many of us get started on home projects and get sidetracked by a little thing called life. A wife. Three kids. A divorce. Whatever. I've been trying to write a book for almost 20 years – and now I finally have! I hope you have enjoyed it.

Printed in the United States
By Bookmasters